Charles Larcom Graves

The Hawarden Horace

Charles Larcom Graves

The Hawarden Horace

ISBN/EAN: 9783337858582

Printed in Europe, USA, Canada, Australia, Japan

Cover: Foto ©ninafisch / pixelio.de

More available books at **www.hansebooks.com**

THE
HAWARDEN HORACE

THE
HAWARDEN HORACE

BY

CHARLES L. GRAVES

AUTHOR OF 'THE BLARNEY BALLADS' 'THE GREEN ABOVE THE RED'

LONDON
SMITH, ELDER, & CO., 15 WATERLOO PLACE
1894

[All rights reserved]

NOTE

TEN of the following pieces have appeared in the columns of the *Spectator*, from which they are reprinted by the kind permission of the editor. The remainder are now published for the first time. The rendering of *Eheu fugaces* (Od. II. 14) is from the pen of Mr. M. H. Temple, and that of *Est mihi nonum* (Od. IV. 11) by Mr. E. V. Lucas. For permission to include their unpublished versions in my collection, as well as for many emendations and helpful suggestions, I desire most cordially and gratefully to acknowledge my indebtedness to these two friends.

C. L. G.

CONTENTS

	PAGE
AD PLANTAGENISTAM	3
AD HIBERNIAM	9
AD MORLEIUM	15
AD ASTROLOGIÆ AMATOREM	21
AD AMICUM	23
AD ARISTIDEN OBFUSCATUM	27
AD CYRILLUM FLOSCULUM	33
AD VERITATIS CULTOREM	37
AD CICERONEM NOSTRUM	41
AD MILESIUM GLORIOSUM	47
AD POSTREMUM GENGULPHUM	53
AD PRIMULAM VULGAREM	57
AD CRŒSUM CHICAGINENSEM	65
CARMEN AMŒBÆUM	71
AD CÆCILIUM AFRICANUM	79
AD DOROTHEAM	87

THE
HAWARDEN HORACE

AD MÆCENATEM

MÆCENAS atavis edite regibus,
O et præsidium et dulce decus meum,
Sunt quos curriculo pulverem Olympicum
Collegisse juvat, metaque fervidis
Evitata rotis palmaque nobilis
Terrarum dominos evehit ad deos ;
Hunc, si mobilium turba Quiritium
Certat tergeminis tollere honoribus ;
Illum, si proprio condidit horreo,
Quidquid de Libycis verritur arcis.
Gaudentem patrio findere sarculo
Agros Attalicis conditionibus

AD PLANTAGENISTAM

Vernon, whose lion port and stately grace
Proclaim thee scion of a royal race !
Vernon, my strenuous henchman, stout and true,
Hast marked the diverse aims that men pursue ?
Some straddling hunchbacked o'er the 'scorching' wheel
In record-cutting all their joyance feel,
Or hold the bounding prowess of a Fry
Exalts the happy athlete to the sky.
Others, again, before the masses bow,
And spend their time in planning to endow
Each yokel with three acres and a cow.
Others, again, unscrupulous modern Horners,
Find bliss in making corn or cotton corners.

AD MÆCENATEM

Nunquam dimoveas, ut trabe Cypria
Myrtoum pavidus nauta secet mare.
Luctantem Icariis fluctibus Africum
Mercator metuens otium et oppidi
Laudat rura sui; mox reficit rates
Quassas indocilis pauperiem pati.
Est qui nec veteris pocula Massici
Nec partem solido demere de die
Spernit, nunc viridi membra sub arbuto
Stratus, nunc ad aquæ lene caput sacræ.
Multos castra juvant et lituo tubæ
Permixtus sonitus bellaque matribus
Detestata. Manet sub Jove frigido
Venator teneræ conjugis immemor,
Seu visa est catulis cerva fidelibus,

AD PLANTAGENISTAM

The Celts, who hunger for the land in fee,

Let aliens reap the riches of their sea,

While British tars, of wind and wave the sport,

Pray, as they pitch and roll, for any port :

Anon, defiant of a watery doom,

Their iron 'Resolution' they resume.

Some whom I know chase cobwebs from their brain

By quaffing brimming bumpers of champagne :

While others, by capricious fortune tried,

Prefer to 'cultivate their own fireside.'

The soldier's life still yields a potent spell,

Nor risk nor hardship can avail to quell ;

For, spite of Labouchere's parochial view,

Our youth read Kipling, and admire Selous

Sport claims its numerous votaries, who roam,

Regardless of the ties of House or home,

By flood and field, o'er moorland, heath and crag,

Their sole desire to make a goodly bag.

Seu rupit teretes Marsus aper plagas.

Me doctarum hederæ præmia frontium

Dis miscent superis ; me gelidum nemus

Nympharumque leves cum Satyris chori

Secernunt populo, si neque tibias

Euterpe cohibet nec Polyhymnia

Lesboum refugit tendere barbiton.

Quod si me lyricis vatibus inseres,

Sublimi feriam sidera vertice.

Me, late withdrawn from Downing's dusty street

To breezy Brighton's Tusculan retreat,

An ardent aspiration stirs and sways

To win and wear the unawarded bays.

Oh, could I by some sweet and swanlike strain

'Translate' myself unto that 'higher plane'[1]

Where Homer, Tennyson, and Horace reign !—

Oh, then, without one solitary pang,

Could I afford to let Home Rule go hang,

Pardon the Peers, and from my conquering car

Look down with brow elate on *Sun* and *Star* !

---

[1] 'Tennyson's exertions have been on a higher plane of human action than my own. He has worked in a higher field, and his work will be more durable.'—*Speech of Mr. Gladstone at Kirkwall*, September 12, 1883.

AD PYRRHAM

Quis multa gracilis te puer in rosa

Perfusus liquidis urget odoribus

    Grato, Pyrrha, sub antro?

        Cui flavam religas comam

Simplex munditiis? Heu quoties fidem

Mutatosque deos flebit, et aspera

AD HIBERNIAM

Redolent of 'Jockey Club,'
    Pliant as a lath,
Is the boy you now decoy
    Down the primrose path.
Him with neatly braided locks
    Lovingly you lure,
Clad in green, and in your mien
    Studiously demure.

Soon from off the gingerbread
    Vanishes the gilt:
Ere the year be spent and sere
    You will prove a jilt.

Nigris æquora ventis
Emirabitur insolens,

Qui nunc te fruitur credulus aurea,
Qui semper vacuam, semper amabilem
Sperat, nescius auræ
Fallacis ! Miseri quibus

Intentata nites. Me tabula sacer
Votiva paries indicat uvida

Do I blame him? No, not I;—
    Only could a wizard
In your face the symptoms trace
    Of the coming blizzard.

Trusting in your halcyon mood
    Thinks he, simple chiel,
You will bide, whate'er betide,
    Lovable and leal.
When a landsman in a sieve
    Braves the Western gales,
Patrick Jones must have his bones—
    (Davy works for Wales).

Lamentable is the lot
    Of the gilded friend
You bemuse and Hugh Price Hughes
    Labours to amend.

Suspendisse potenti

Vestimenta maris deo.

I was very nearly wrecked
    Rounding Ireland's Eye ;
But I swam, and here I am
    High and dry and spry.

AD PLANCUM

LAUDABUNT alii claram Rhodon aut Mytilenen,
   Aut Epheson bimarisve Corinthi
Mœnia, vel Baccho Thebas vel Apolline Delphos
   Insignes aut Thessala Tempe.
Sunt, quibus unum opus est intactæ Palladis urbem
   Carmine perpetuo celebrare, et

AD MORLEIUM

Some say 'twas in Midlothian, and some there be who swear
I first beheld the moonlight in the wilds of county Clare.
Some say 'twas Tory Island, and some have little doubt
'Twas either Tara famed for song, or Dublin famed for stout.
Some back the Modern Athens, whose architecture's grace
In all its 'virgin purity'[1] in memory I retrace.

[1] 'I know Edinburgh well; I knew almost every street and every corner . . . when Edinburgh was in what I may call the virgin purity of its architecture.' *Speech of Mr. Gladstone at the Council Chamber, Edinburgh*, November 25, 1879.

Undique decerptam fronti præponere olivam.
Plurimus in Junonis honorem
Aptum dicet equis Argos ditesque Mycenas.
Me nec tam patiens Lacedæmon
Nec tam Larissæ percussit campus opimæ,
Quam domus Albuneæ resonantis
Et præceps Anio ac Tiburni lucus et uda
Mobilibus pomaria rivis.
Albus ut obscuro deterget nubila cœlo
Sæpe Notus neque parturit imbres
Perpetuos, sic tu sapiens finire memento
Tristitiam vitæque labores

AD MORLEIUM

Hall Caine would like to claim me for the Isle of Grand
    Old Man,
And Labouchere's disposed to think I hail from the
    Soudan ;
While many a gallant Taffy is as sure as eggs can be
That from the house of Harlech I derive my pedigree.
But though unable to affirm that I have not been
    smitten
With all the disadvantages of being born a Briton,
In spite of strong inducements to emerge on alien earth
I blush to own in Liverpool the background of my birth.
But stay, I'll move the closure here.

                        Though, Morley, you and I
Were born and bred on English soil, 'neath England's
    foggy sky,
Though wearied by your daily dose of endless Irish
    stew,
Though Art is looking Yellow, and politics look blue,

Molli, Plance, mero, seu te fulgentia signis
  Castra tenent seu densa tenebit
Tiburis umbra tui. Teucer Salamina patremque
  Quum fugeret, tamen uda Lyæo
Tempora populea fertur vinxisse corona,
  Sic tristes affatus amicos :
' Quo nos cunque feret melior fortuna parente
  Ibimus, o socii comitesque !
Nil desperandum Teucro duce et auspice Teucro ;
  Certus enim promisit Apollo,
Ambiguam tellure nova Salamina futuram.
  O fortes pejoraque passi
Mecum sæpe viri, nunc vino pellite curas ;
  Cras ingens iterabimus æquor.'

Like me forget your troubles for a while, bid care avaunt.

Take tickets for the pantomine, or visit 'Charley's Aunt.'

Remember how in '65, when Dizzy's craft abhorred

Induced my *alma mater* to throw me overboard—

Did I assume the willow, or cringe beneath the blow,

Or bid my sad supporters an eternal farewell? No!

I shook the dust of Oxford from my feet and sallied forth

And in two days was sitting for a county in the North.

'Cheer up, faint-hearted Liberals!'—so rang my clarion cry—

' At last I am unmuzzled : never think of saying die !

What though my foster parent has ejected me in scorn,

I'm certain of a welcome in the shire where I was born.

Once more the flowing tide is ours ; be brave and banish sorrow,

What Lancashire decides to-day is England's will to-morrow.'

AD LEUCONOËN

Tu ne quæsieris, scire nefas, quem mihi, quem tibi
Finem di dederint, Leuconoë, nec Babylonios
Tentaris numeros. Ut melius, quidquid erit, pati !
Seu plures hiemes seu tribuit Jupiter ultimam,
Quæ nunc oppositis debilitat pumicibus mare
Tyrrhenum, sapias, vina liques et spatio brevi
Spem longam reseces. Dum loquimur, fugerit invida
Ætas. Carpe diem quam minimum credula postero.

AD ASTROLOGIÆ AMATOREM

Dear Mr. Stead, excuse me if I beg you, as a friend,
To cease importuning the spooks about my latter end.
Your Babylonish numbers, I admit, were even worse,
But still, a taste for spirits is undoubtedly a curse.
Far better leave the stars alone, and, banishing to Burmah
Your astral misalliances, take root on *terra firma*.
This chilly June may be our last, or Providence decree
That we shall both contribute to the *Twentieth Century*.
In either case try drinking port, and study to be sane,
Lest your high hopes should ruin down the limitless inane.
E'en as I write this post-card, time flies, hand over hand:
Then cultivate the daily press, nor trust in *Borderland*.

AD MÆCENATEM

Vile potabis modicis Sabinum
Cantharis, Græca quod ego ipse testa
Conditum levi, datus in theatro
    Cum tibi plausus,

Care Mæcenas eques, ut paterni
Fluminis ripæ simul et jocosa
Redderet laudes tibi Vaticani
    Montis imago.

Cæcubum et prelo domitam Caleno
Tu bibes uvam : mea nec Falernæ

AD AMICUM

DEAR Acton, next Wednesday, at dinner,
    I cannot but honestly think
You'll find that my claret is thinner
    Than that you're accustomed to drink.
Twelve shillings a dozen it cost me
    That year—I remember it well—
When Oxford, that loved me yet lost me,
    Created you Hon. D.C.L.

The cheers by your presence excited
    That filled the Sheldonian dome,
The Vatican vastly delighted,
    And sensibly gratified Rome.

Temperant vites neque Formiani
Pocula colles.

And so, for the savour historic
    That clings to my modest Bordeaux,
You'll pardon its want of caloric,
    And vote it the choicest of Clos.

AD ARISTIUM FUSCUM

INTEGER vitæ scelerisque purus
Non eget Mauris jaculis neque arcu
Nec venenatis gravida sagittis,
    Fusce, pharetra,

Sive per Syrtes iter æstuosas
Sive facturus per inhospitalem
Caucasum vel quæ loca fabulosus
    Lambit Hydaspes.

Namque me silva lupus in Sabina,
Dum meam canto Lalagen et ultra

AD ARISTIDEN OBFUSCATUM

IF clear be your conscience, my Morley,
   No bullet-proof coat you'll require,
Though often dispirited sorely
   By Erin's Invincible ire:
Nay further, discarding coercion,
   You may with impunity fare
On a midsummer moonlight excursion
   Unarmed through the County of Clare.

Look at me. As the breeze of the zephyr
   I strolled forth of late to enjoy,
A vicious and virulent heifer—
   I was humming the 'Dear Irish Boy'—

Terminum curis vagor expeditis,
Fugit inermem,

Quale portentum neque militaris
Daunias latis alit æsculetis
Nec Jubæ tellus generat, leonum
Arida nutrix.

Pone me pigris ubi nulla campis
Arbor æstiva recreatur aura,

AD ARISTIDEN OBFUSCATUM

Came fiercely galumphing beside me :
But suddenly changing its tone,
The animal amiably eyed me,
And left me severely alone.

O wild is Hibernia's Taurus,
And Collings' chimerical cow,
And neither demure nor decorous
Is the Tammany Bos, but I vow
That even in Chamberlain's garden [1]
No wickeder brute you'll espy
Than the horrible heifer of Hawarden,
Who fled from my emerald eye.

Were I bound within range of a rifle
In Dopping's implacable grip ;

---

[1] On May 7, 1894, Mr. Austen Chamberlain, M.P., was gored by a Guernsey bull at Highbury.

Quod latus mundi nebulæ malusque

    Jupiter urget :

Pone sub curru nimium propinqui

Solis in terra domibus negata :

Dulce ridentem Lalagen amabo,

    Dulce loquentem.

AD ARISTIDEN OBFUSCATUM

Though I fled to the summit of Eiffel
    To give Ashmead-Bartlett the slip ;
Were I doomed to despair on Sahara,
    Or sentenced to dine with the Shah,
Still I'd chant, to the tune of Ta-ra-ra,
    The praises of Erin-go-Bragh.

AD PUERUM

Persicos odi, puer, apparatus,
Displicent nexæ philyra coronæ ;
Mitte sectari, rosa quo locorum
    Sera moretur.

Simplici myrto nihil allabores
Sedulus curo : neque te ministrum

AD CYRILLUM FLOSCULUM

Oriental flowers, my Cyril,
   (Save of language) I detest:
Cull for me no costly orchid
   To adorn my blameless breast.
Nor essay to deck my raiment
   With the blushing English rose,
For its brutal Saxon odour
   Aggravates my Scottish nose.

Me as Minister the fragrance
   Of the leek doth most arride,
With the shamrock and the thistle
   In a triple posy tied :

Dedecet myrtus, neque me sub arcta

Vite bibentem.

So, beneath my grand umbrella
    Firmly fixed on College Green,
Let us deviate from duty
    In a deluge of poteen.

AD DELLIUM

Æquam memento rebus in arduis
Servare mentem, non secus in bonis
   Ab insolenti temperatam
     Lætitia, moriture Delli,

Seu mæstus omni tempore vixeris
Seu te in remoto gramine per dies
   Festos reclinatum bearis
     Interiore nota Falerni.

Huc vina et unguenta et nimium breves
Flores amœnæ ferre jube rosæ,
   Dum res et ætas et sororum
     Fila trium patiuntur atra.

AD VERITATIS CULTOREM

Henry, sore shattered by this trying summer,
   Pray keep a level head like mine, nor deign
To play the mad Mephistophelean mummer,
   Should fickle fortune favour us again.

Whether you toil in London like a nigger,
   Or, snatching hurriedly a breathing space,
At some familiar German baths you figure,
   Quaffing the waters with impassive grace,

Scorn not the wine-cup, puff the Melachrino,
   And pluck the pallid Primrose while you may,
Ere Time, that mocks at Holloway and Eno,
   O'er Truth's own editor shall assert his sway.

Cedes coëmptis saltibus et domo
Villaque, flavus quam Tiberis lavit,
    Cedes, et exstructis in altum
    Divitiis potietur heres.

Divesne prisco natus ab Inacho,
Nil interest, an pauper et infima
    De gente sub divo moreris,
    Victima nil miserantis Orci.

Omnes eodem cogimur, omnium
Versatur urna serius ocius
    Sors exitura et nos in æternum
    Exsilium impositura cymbæ.

For there will come an hour when you, my Labby,
    Must quit your charming villa and your lands
At Twickenham, and (resting in the Abbey)
    Bequeath your modest pile to other hands.

What though to noble Frenchmen famed in story
    You trace your blood's cerulean tint, I fear
The least sophisticated rural Tory
    In mere longevity may prove your peer.

Death waits on all, impartial, unrelenting,
    And none of mortals may the summons brave
That bids us, or resigned or unconsenting,
    Fare forth upon th' irremeable wave.

AD SEPTIMIUM

Septimi, Gades aditure mecum et
Cantabrum indoctum juga ferre nostra et
Barbaras Syrtes, ubi Maura semper
 Æstuat unda ;

Tibur Argeo positum colono
Sit meæ sedes utinam senectæ,
Sit modus lasso maris et viarum
 Militiæque !

AD CICERONEM NOSTRUM

MAJESTIC Armitstead, colossal crony,
    Ever at shortest notice all agog
To start for Brighton as my cicerone,
    For Gothenburg, Khartoum, or Ballybog—
Prepared, did Arctic fever fire my soul,
To pilot me in person to the Pole !

A truce, old friend, to Continental touring :
    Tempt me no more in foreign realms to roam :
To me incomparably more alluring
    Are the delights of Hawarden and of home :
For I have crowded more into my span
Than any mortal since the Ithacan.

Unde si Parcæ prohibent iniquæ,
Dulce pellitis ovibus Galæsi
Flumen et regnata petam Laconi
Rura Phalanto.

Ille terrarum mihi præter omnes
Angulus ridet, ubi non Hymetto
Mella decedunt viridique certat
Bacca Venafro.

Ver ubi longum tepidasque præbet
Jupiter brumas, et amicus Aulon

Thence if the savage Sassenach should hound me
  Into the heart of gallant little Wales,
O may some suitable retreat be found me
  Amid fair Cambria's enchanting vales ;
For I have ever been, and am, a glutton
For all things Welsh—from music down to mutton.

Yes, Wales I love, home of the bilious bunny ;
  Home of my fiery namesake, Mr. Gee ;
Whose heather yields the most delicious honey,
  Whose Bards are countless as the sands o' Dee.
Whose leek, to any educated nose,
Is sweeter than the overrated rose.

There, to assuage the thirsty native throttle,
  My noble and accomplished friend Lord Bute [1]

---

[1] In South Wales, Lord Bute has had a vineyard for nineteen years, and he has made good wine from his grapes. Lord Bute's

Fertili Baccho minimum Falernis
Invidet uvis.

Ille te mecum locus et beatæ
Postulant arces ; ibi tu calentem
Debita sparges lacrima favillam
Vatis amici

Grows splendid wine at nine-and-six the bottle—

A most refined and lucrative pursuit.

In fact, there's not 'the differ of' a *bouton*

'Twixt Mouton Rothschild and this Cymru Mouton

There Watkin's high but hospitable châlet

Will oftentimes invite us for a climb

By slow and easy stages from the valley,

To hoary Snowdon's pinnacle sublime

There let us live and die, and dying, win

Meet elegy from Morris of Penbryn.

head gardener says that some of the wine from the 1881 crop realised 115*s*. a dozen when sold by auction at Birmingham last year. This crop was grown at Castell Coch. Lord Bute has now another large vineyard on the shore of the Bristol Channel, where the 'Gamy Nori' grapes last year gave forty hogsheads of wine of the best quality.' *Daily Graphic*, September 17, 1894.

AD LICINIUM MURENAM

RECTIUS vives, Licini, neque altum
Semper urgendo neque, dum procellas
Cautus horrescis, nimium premendo
    Litus iniquum.

Auream quisquis mediocritatem
Diligit, tutus caret obsoleti
Sordibus tecti, caret invidenda
    Sobrius aula.

AD MILESIUM GLORIOSUM

'Twould please me greatly, dear Tay Pay.
If from exaggeration's sway
    You could be weaned.
I m not, although you'd have it so,
A perfect seraph, nor is ' Joe '
    A perfect fiend.

The pressman who in all his prose
' Conspicuous moderation ' shows,
    Can never fill
A place upon the Birthday lists,
Nor sink, 'mid hireling eulogists,
    To puff a pill.

AD LICINIUM MURENAM

Sæpius ventis agitatur ingens

Pinus, et celsæ graviore casu

Decidunt turres, feriuntque summos

Fulgura montes.

Sperat infestis, metuit secundis

Alteram sortem bene præparatum

Pectus. Informes hiemes reducit

Jupiter, idem

Summovet. Non, si male nunc, et olim

Sic erit. Quondam cithara tacentem

Balloons that soar to heights unknown,
An ugly way at times have shown
    Of going pop :
And you, Sol's charioteer-in-chief,
Must face, if e'er you come to grief,
    A long, long drop.

When fickle fortune wears a frown,
Be not dis-astrously cast down ;
    Nor trust her smile :
The Sun, we know, can't always shine ;
But then, last June was quite as fine
    As this is vile.

Although the outlook's somewhat black,
With Rosebery on Ladas' back
    'Tis bound to mend ;

Suscitat musam neque semper arcum

Tendit Apollo.

Rebus angustis animosus atque

Fortis appare; sapienter idem

Contrahes vento nimium secundo

Turgida vela

AD MILESIUM GLORIOSUM

When Tara's harp is heard anew,
Your editorial long-bow you
    May well unbend.

Though our majorities be small,
And candid friends predict our fall,
    Tay Pay, sit tight;
Refraining, when we gaily glide
Upon the fair and flowing tide,
    From blatherskite.

AD POSTUMUM

Eheu fugaces, Postume, Postume,
Labuntur anni nec pietas moram
    Rugis et instanti senectæ
        Afferet indomitæque morti :

Non, si trecenis, quotquot eunt dies,
Amice, places illacrimabilem
    Plutona tauris, qui ter amplum
        Geryonen Tityonque tristi

Compescit unda, scilicet omnibus,
Quicunque terræ munere vescimur,
    Enaviganda, sive reges
        Sive inopes erimus coloni.

AD POSTREMUM GENGULPHUM

AH, Ellis, Ellis! Waning fame
    Nor art nor eloquence can stay;
A dog, though hyphened be his name,
    Can only have his day.

Though up and down the country you
    Should daily thump three hundred tubs,
You would not soothe the Marquess, who
    Rollit and Randolph snubs.

The common lot! We all at last
    Receive the inevitable sack—
The Jingo, the Iconoclast,
    The Peer, the Party Hack.

Frustra cruento Marte carebimus
Fractisque rauci fluctibus Hadriae,
   Frustra per autumnos nocentem
      Corporibus metuemus Austrum :

Visendus ater flumine languido
Cocytus errans et Danai genus
   Infame damnatusque longi
      Sisyphus Æolides laboris.

Linquenda tellus et domus et placens
Uxor, neque harum, quas colis, arborum
   Te præter invisas cupressos
      Ulla brevem dominum sequetur.

Absumet heres Cæcuba dignior
Servata centum clavibus et mero
   Tinget pavimentum superbo,
      Pontificum potiore coenis.

In vain to murderous war you urge
   The armies of the Empress Queen,
In vain her navies o'er the surge
     You steer to College Green:

Below the gangway must you sit
   With Bartley, Hanbury, and Bowles;
A mark for journalistic wit,
     A butt for all the Souls.

No Civil Lordship then for you;
   England, your love, will disappear;
The *North American Review*
     Alone your cry will hear.

Another patriot will arise,
   A bolder guardian of the Guelph,
A coiner of more raucous cries,
     More blatant than yourself.

AD GROSPHUM

Otium divos rogat in patenti
Prensus Ægæo, simul atra nubes
Condidit lunam neque certa fulgent
    Sidera nautis;

Otium bello furiosa Thrace,
Otium Medi pharetra decori,
Grosphe, non gemmis neque purpura ve-
    nale neque auro.

Non enim gazæ neque consularis
Summovet lictor miseros tumultus
Mentis et curas laqueata circum
    Tecta volantes.

AD PRIMULAM VULGAREM

CALM upon the broad Atlantic, tossed by billows fierce
    and frantic,
  Pallid passengers inordinately crave,
As the angry ocean surges and the sire of Boanerges
    Cataclysmically merges cloud and wave.

Calm it is that wan advisers of unconscionable Kaisers
    Unceasingly are striving to attain—
Calm, the coveted of Chilians and belligerent Brazilians,
    Calm, that even Mackay's millions court in vain.

For although your wealth be teeming far beyond a miser's
    dreaming,
  Though your lackeys have the lustre of Lord Mayors,
Pomp affords no mitigation of the cankering vexation
    Of a democrat condemned to sit upstairs.

Vivitur parvo bene, cui paternum
Splendet in mensa tenui salinum,
Nec leves somnos timor aut cupido
Sordidus aufert.

Quid brevi fortes jaculamur ævo
Multa? Quid terras alio calentes
Sole mutamus? Patriæ quis exsul
Se quoque fugit?

Scandit æratas vitiosa naves
Cura nec turmas equitum relinquit,
Ocior cervis et agente nimbos
Ocior Euro.

AD PRIMULAM VULGAREM

Modest wants are soonest sated; though their spoons be
    silver-plated,
  Many men by sounder slumbers are restored
Than if they yearly spent more than the millionaire of
    Mentmore,
  Or drank from golden goblets like a lord.

What avails our ceaseless striving, planning, plotting, and
    contriving,
  As we flit in search of sunshine or of peace
To the heart of Cochin-China, Carolina, Argentina?
  Even Liberators can't obtain release.

Care asserts her odious power in the warship's conning-
    tower,
  Scruples not the gilded guardsman to assail;
And her onset far surpasses e'en such speed as Isinglass's,
  Surpasses e'en the racers of the rail.

Lætus in præsens animus quod ultra est
Oderit curare et amara lento
Temperet risu.   Nihil est ab omni
    Parte beatum.

Abstulit clarum cita mors Achillem,
Longa Tithonum minuit senectus,
Et mihi forsan, tibi quod negarit,
    Porriget hora.

Te greges centum Siculæque circum
Mugiunt vaccæ, tibi tollit hinnitum

To anticipate disaster brings it hitherward the faster;
   Oh, believe me, Tapley's attitude is best.
As for Labouchere's reviling, learn from me to bear it smiling:
   No lot on earth is altogether blest.

Canning's doom was brilliant brevity; ineffectual longevity
   Obscured the early eminence of Grey:
And it may be in our sequel, though in length of span unequal,
   Serener joys shall crown my closing day.

You have parks as broad as prairies, you've Elizabethan dairies,[1]
   You've an army of retainers at your call:

---

[1] 'Mentmore, "the lordly pleasure house" which the Earl of Rosebery came into possession of on his marriage, is celebrated far

Apta quadrigis equa, te bis Afro

Murice tinctæ

Vestiunt lanæ: mihi parva rura et

Spiritum Graiæ tenuem Camenæ

Parca non mendax dedit et malignum

Spernere vulgus.

And the winner of the 'Guineas' and the Derby proudly
 whinnies
Whene'er the Opposition has a fall.

I've a small estate at Hawarden, with a nice old-fashioned
 garden,
I've a pair of carriage-horses and a cob ;
And I con my classic folios far from Parliament's im-
 broglios,
Unembarrassed by the mandate of the mob.

and wide for its noble halls and beautiful gardens. . . . Lord Rosebery's is essentially a dairy farm. . . . The dairy is . . . provo-
cative of admiration, with its Elizabethan architecture. . . . In
the centre is a marble fountain. . . . . On the wooden shelves is a
good deal of china, chiefly in Dresden and other fine ware. . . . .
The orchard is under the jurisdiction of Mr. J. Smith, who has fifty
gardeners and labourers under his direction.' From ' The Prime
Minister as Farmer,' *Westminster Gazette*, April 25, 1894.

DE CONTINENTIA

Non ebur neque aureum
   Mea renidet in domo lacunar,
Non trabes Hymettiæ
   Premunt columnas ultima recisas
Africa, neque Attali
   Ignotus heres regiam occupavi,
Nec Laconicas mihi
   Trahunt honestæ purpuras clientæ :
At fides et ingeni
   Benigna vena est, pauperemque dives
Me petit ; nihil supra
   Deos lacesso nec potentem amicum

AD CRŒSUM CHICAGINENSEM

No staircase of marble, no ceiling
By Tadema painted, are mine ;
My spoons are unworthy of stealing,
No epicure envies my wine.
No millionaire ever bequeathed me
The tithe of his riches untold,
Nor has any Tracy enwreathed me,
Like Dizzy, with laurels of gold

No, mine is an intellect spacious,
A record unsullied by blame,
And even Carnegie is gracious
Enough my acquaintance to claim

Largiora flagito

    Satis beatus unicis Sabinis.

Truditur dies die,

    Novæque pergunt interire lunæ.

Tu secanda marmora

    Locas sub ipsum funus et sepulcri

Immemor struis domos

    Marisque Baiis obstrepentis urges

Summovere litora,

    Parum locuples continente ripa.

Quid, qued usque proximos

    Revellis agri terminos et ultra

Limites clientium

    Salis avarus? Pellitur paternos

In sinu ferens deos

    Et uxor et vir sordidosque natos.

AD CRŒSUM CHICAGINENSEM

Heav'n's bounty for naught I importune,
 I cringe not to rich or to great,
Supremely content with my fortune,
 My snug little Flintshire estate.

Though time, like Niagara speeding,
 Brings doom to the plutocrat peer,
Of death and its duties unheeding
 New palaces hastes he to rear.
Or, craving a keener emotion
 Than life on the mainland supplies,
He scours o'er the surface of ocean
 In yachts of extravagant size.

Nay more if he thinks that his shooting
 The huts of the husbandmen spoil,
He never refrains from uprooting
 Poor tenants by scores from the soil:

Nulla certior tamen
Rapacis Orci fine destinata
Aula divitem manet
Herum. Quid ultra tendis? Æqua tellus
Pauperi recluditur
Regumque pueris, nec satelles Orci
Callidum Promethea
Revexit auro captus. Hic superbum
Tantalum atque Tantali
Genus coërcet, hic levare functum
Pauperem laboribus
Vocatus atque non vocatus audit.

For, sifting the facts from the fictions—
　　A duty no sage should refuse—
'Twixt Scottish and Irish evictions
　　There isn't a penny to choose.

Yet Harcourt, that resolute wrecker,
　　Whose *fiat* we humbly obey,
To fatten his famished exchequer
　　Marks down even Dukes for his prey!
In vain his remorseless exaction
　　They daily endeavour to dodge;
Death's sole and supreme satisfaction
　　Is tasted by penniless Hodge.

CARMEN AMŒBÆUM

Hor.   Donec gratus eram tibi,
Nec quisquam potior brachia candidæ
Cervici juvenis dabat,
Persarum vigui rege beatior.

Lyd.   Donec non alia magis
Arsisti, neque erat Lydia post Chloën,

CARMEN AMŒBÆUM

Will. When in the golden days of yore
  Thy favour I enjoyed
(Though purely Scottish to the core).
  My bliss was unalloyed :
Proud of a love that jealous fate
  Methought could never mar,
I envied not the high estate
  Of Kaiser or of Czar.

Brit. So long, sweet William, as I reigned
  Unrivalled in thy breast,
Ere blarneying Hibernia gained
  The throne I erst possessed ;

CARMEN AMOEBAEUM

Multi Lydia nominis
Romana vigui clarior Ilia.

Hor. Me nunc Thressa Chloë regit
Dulces docta modos et citharæ sciens,
Pro qua non metuam mori,
Si parcent animæ fata superstiti.

Lyd. Me torret face mutua
Thurini Calaïs filius Ornyti,

Proud of thy genius and thy love,
   I candidly confess
I ranked Victoria's realm above
   The realm of good Queen Bess.

Will. Me now Hibernia holds in thrall,
   My crownless harpy Queen !
With her I chant in Tara's Hall
   ' The Wearing of the Green.'
For her dear sake I'd rant and rail
   At every institution,
Although such conduct should entail
   A sudden dissolution.

Brit. Me Cecil fires with mutual flame,
   My masterful *Marquis* !
I love him for his noble name,
   His ancient pedigree.

Pro quo bis patiar mori,
Si parcent puero fata superstiti.

Hor. Quid, si prisca redit Venus,
Diductosque jugo cogit aëneo?
Si flava excutitur Chloë,
Rejectæque patet janua Lydiæ?

Lyd. Quanquam sidere pulchrior
Ille est, tu levior cortice et improbo

Two dissolutions in two years
    For him I'd undergo,
Provided that the House of Peers
    Escaped an overthrow.

Will. Suppose the old familiar fire
    Afresh within me burned?
Suppose the lady and her lyre
    In weariness I spurned?
What if I bowed my Irish bride
    Politely to the door,
And swore unswervingly to bide
    With thee for evermore?

Brit. Though fairer than the *Star* were he,
    Than Hottentot thou sabler,
More flighty than Mid-Cork's M.P.,
    Than Channel chops unstabler,

Iracundior Hadria,

Tecum vivere amem, tecum obeam libens.

CARMEN AMŒBÆUM

With thee as guardian of my race
    Life's bliss anew would bloom,
With thee unfalteringly I'd face
    The deadly ding of doom.

AD MÆCENATEM

INCLUSAM Danaën turris aënea
Robustæque fores et vigilum canum
Tristes excubiæ munierant satis
    Nocturnis ab adulteris,
Si non Acrisium virginis abditæ
Custodem pavidum Jupiter et Venus
Risissent: fore enim tutum iter et patens
    Converso in pretium deo.
Aurum per medios ire satellites
Et perrumpere amat saxa potentius

AD CÆCILIUM AFRICANUM

Girt round by scrub and stream, and closely guarded
　By valiant warriors waiting on his call,
Loben the brave, who erst the lean earth larded,
　Were even now at peace within his kraal,
Holding unchallenged sway o'er his possessions,
　Meting rude justice both to young and old,
But for the craze for claims and for concessions,
　But for the over-mastering greed of gold.

Gold saps the moral fibre of electors,
　Lures building companies from virtue's way.

Ictu fulmineo: concidit auguris

Argivi domus ob lucrum

Demersa exitio; diffidit urbium

Portas vir Macedo et subruit æmulos

Reges muneribus; munera navium

Sævos illaqueant duces.

Crescentem sequitur cura pecuniam

Majorumque fames. Jure perhorrui

Late conspicuum tollere verticem,

Mæcenas, equitum decus.

Quanto quisque sibi plura negaverit,

Ab dis plura feret: nil cupientium

Nudus castra peto et transfuga divitum

Partes linquere gestio,

Demoralises deputies, directors,
 And brings the house of Jabez to decay.
Gold tempts the skippers of a neutral nation
 To run the fearful perils of blockade ;
Gold was the means of Erin's degradation,
 When Pitt his 'blackguard' policy essayed.

Wealth, as it waxes, only brings vexation,
 Linked with a never-ceasing thirst for pelf :
Happy is he, who, shunning speculation,
 Remains a simple commoner, like myself.
The life of self-denial far surpasses
 The 'cushioned ease'[1] of dukes and millionaires,
And I have found more virtue in the masses
 Than in the cleanest class who purchase Pears'.

---

[1] 'It is possible that he [Mr. Chamberlain] may have a cer tain enjoyment in the cushioned ease of that society in which he now mixes with satisfaction.'—*Speech of Mr. Gladstone at the Memorial Hall*, London, July 29, 1887.

Contemptæ dominus splendidior rei,
Quam si quidquid arat impiger Apulus
Occultare meis dicerer horreis,
    Magnas inter opes inops.
Puræ rivus aquæ silvaque jugerum
Paucorum et segetis certa fides meæ
Fulgentem imperio fertilis Africæ
    Fallit sorte beatior.
Quanquam nec Calabræ mella ferunt apes
Nec Læstrygonia Bacchus in amphora
Languescit mihi nec pinguia Gallicis
    Crescunt vellera pascuis,
Importuna tamen pauperies abest
Nec, si plura velim, tu dare deneges.

Leader of these, I harbour no ambition
    To own a gold reef, or control De Beers :
My small estate in Wales, my Irish mission,
    Suffice to solace my declining years.
Such is the bliss for which alone I hunger ;
    So dowered, I would not, were the option free,
Exchange with you, though forty summers younger,
    And lord of Africa from sea to sea.

Tis true no dainties deck my frugal table ;
    I don't possess a dozen of Lafite ;
I own no cattle-ranche nor racing stable,
    Nor do my yachts with 'Vigilant' compete.
But I am far removed from destitution,
    Far from the 'Union,' whatsoe'er betide ;
And, judging by your famous contribution,
    More, if I wanted it, you would provide.

Contracto melius parva cupidine
    Vectigalia porrigam,
Quam si Mygdoniis regnum Alyattei
Campis continuem.   Multa petentibus
Desunt multa: bene est, cui deus obtulit
    Parca, quod satis est, manu.

Take it from me— no philosophic tyro—
　　Happier the man who limits his desires,
Than he who prances from Cape Town to Cairo,
　　Or spans the wastes of Africa with wires.
Excessive wants on earth are never sated,
　　Nor mines nor millions avarice can assuage:
Blest he, from Income-tax emancipated,
　　Who is content to earn a living wage.

AD PHYLLIDEM

Est mihi nonum superantis annum
Plenus Albani cadus; est in horto,
Phylli, nectendis apium coronis;
    Est hederæ vis
Multa, qua crines religata fulges;
Ridet argento domus; ara castis
Vincta verbenis avet immolato
    Spargier agno;
Cuncta festinat manus, huc et illuc
Cursitant mixtæ pueris puellæ;
Sordidum flammæ trepidant rotantes
    Vertice fumum.

AD DOROTHEAM

I know where there is honey in a jar
    Meet for a certain little friend of mine ;
And, Dorothy, I know where daisies are
    That only wait small hands to intertwine
    A wreath for such a golden head as thine.

The thought that thou art coming makes all glad :
    The house is bright with blossoms high and low,
And many a little lass and little lad
    Expectantly are running to and fro :
    The fire within our hearts is all aglow.

Ut tamen noris quibus advoceris
Gaudiis, Idus tibi sunt agendæ,
Qui dies mensem Veneris marinæ
    Findit Aprilem,
Jure sollemnis mihi sanctiorque
Pæne natali proprio, quod ex hac
Luce Mæcenas meus adfluentes
    Ordinat annos.
Telephum, quem tu petis, occupavit
Non tuæ sortis juvenem puella
Dives et lasciva tenetque grata
    Compede vinctum.
Terret ambustus Phaëthon avaras
Spes, et exemplum grave præbet ales
Pegasus terrenum equitem gravatus
    Bellerophontem,
Semper ut te digna sequare et ultra
Quam licet sperare nefas putando

AD DOROTHEAM

We want thee, child, to share in our delight
   On this high day, the holiest and best,
Because 'twas then, ere youth had taken flight,
   Thy grandmamma, of women loveliest,
   Made me of men most honoured and most blest.

That haughty boy who led thee to suppose
   He was thy sweetheart, has, I grieve to tell,
Been seen to pick the garden's choicest rose
   And toddle with it to another belle,
   Who does not treat him altogether well.

But mind not that, or let it teach thee this—
   To waste no love on any youthful rover
(All youths are rovers, I assure thee, Miss).
   No, if thou wouldst true constancy discover,
   Thy grandpapa is perfect as a lover.

Disparem vites. Age jam meorum
  Finis amorum—
Non enim posthac alia calebo
Femina—condisce modos amanda
Voce quos reddas; minuentur atræ
  Carmine curæ.

AD DOROTHEAM

So come, thou playmate of my closing day,
  The latest treasure life can offer me,
And with thy baby laughter make us gay.
  Thy fresh young voice shall sing, my Dorothy,
Songs that shall bid the feet of sorrow flee.

SMITH, ELDER, & CO.'S PUBLICATIONS.

THE WHITE COMPANY. By A. CONAN DOYLE, Author of 'Micah Clarke' &c. Thirteenth Edition. Crown 8vo. 6s.

STANHOPE OF CHESTER: a Mystery. By PERCY ANDREAE. Crown 8vo. 6s.

GRANIA: the Story of an Island. By the Hon. EMILY LAWLESS. Crown 8vo. 3s. 6d.

MARCELLA. By Mrs. HUMPHRY WARD, Author of 'Robert Elsmere' &c. Popular Edition. Crown 8vo. 6s.

THE HISTORY OF DAVID GRIEVE. By Mrs. HUMPHRY WARD, Author of 'Robert Elsmere' &c. Popular Edition, crown 8vo. 6s. Cheap Edition, crown 8vo. limp cloth, 2s. 6d.

ROBERT ELSMERE. By Mrs. HUMPHRY WARD, Author of 'Marcella,' 'The History of David Grieve,' &c. Popular Edition, crown 8vo. 6s.; CHEAP EDITION, crown 8vo. limp cloth, 2s. 6d.; Cabinet Edition, 2 vols. small 8vo. 12s.

THE GAMEKEEPER AT HOME; or, Sketches of Natural History, Poaching, and Rural Life. By RICHARD JEFFERIES. With Illustrations. Crown 8vo. 5s.

By the same Author.

WILD LIFE IN A SOUTHERN COUNTY. Crown 8vo. 6s.

THE AMATEUR POACHER. Crown 8vo. 5s.

HODGE AND HIS MASTERS. Crown 8vo. 7s. 6d.

ROUND ABOUT A GREAT ESTATE. Crown 8vo. 5s.

WOODLAND, MOOR, AND STREAM; being the Notes of a Naturalist. Edited by J. A. OWEN. Second Edition. Crown 8vo. 5s.

FOREST TITHES; and other Studies from Nature. By the Author of 'Woodland, Moor, and Stream,' &c. Edited by J. A. OWEN. Crown 8vo. 5s.

ALL THE YEAR WITH NATURE. By P. ANDERSON GRAHAM. Crown 8vo. 5s.

A PAIR OF LOVERS; and other Tales. 'The Short and Simple Annals of the Poor.' By IDA LEMON. Crown 8vo. 4s. 6d.

WHAT OUR DAUGHTERS CAN DO FOR THEMSELVES: a Handbook of Women's Employments. By Mrs. H. COLEMAN DAVIDSON, Author of 'Dainties: English and Foreign,' 'Eggs,' &c. Crown 8vo. 3s. 6d.

A BRIDE FROM THE BUSH. By E. W. HORNUNG. Crown 8vo. limp red cloth, 2s. 6d.

JESS. By H. RIDER HAGGARD, Author of 'King Solomon's Mines' &c. Crown 8vo. limp red cloth, 2s. 6d.

VICE VERSÂ; or, a Lesson to Fathers. By F. ANSTEY. Crown 8vo. limp red cloth, 2s. 6d.

By the same Author.

A FALLEN IDOL. Crown 8vo. 6s. Cheap Edition, crown 8vo. limp red cloth, 2s. 6d.

THE PARIAH. Crown 8vo. 6s. Cheap Edition, crown 8vo. limp red cloth, 2s. 6d.

THE GIANT'S ROBE. Crown 8vo. 6s. Cheap Edition, crown 8vo. limp red cloth, 2s. 6d.

THE TALKING HORSE, and other Tales. Crown 8vo. 6s. Cheap Edition, cr. 8vo. limp red cloth, 2s. 6d.

MORE T LEAVES; a Collection of Pieces for Public Reading. By EDWARD F. TURNER, Author of 'T Leaves,' 'Tantler's Sister,' &c. Cr. 8vo. 4s. 6d.

By the same Author.

T LEAVES; a Collection of Pieces for Public Reading. Sixth Edition. Crown 8vo. 3s. 6d.

TANTLER'S SISTER; AND OTHER UNTRUTHFUL STORIES: being a Collection of Pieces written for Public Reading. Third Edition. Crown 8vo. 3s. 6d.

London: SMITH, ELDER, & CO., 15 Waterloo Place.

SMITH, ELDER, & CO.'S PUBLICATIONS.

A SHORT HISTORY OF THE RENAISSANCE IN ITALY. Taken from the work of John Addington Symonds. By Lieut.-Col. Alfred Pearson. With a Steel Engraving of a recent Portrait of Mr. Symonds. Demy 8vo. 12s. 6d.

VOLTAIRE'S VISIT TO ENGLAND, 1726-1729. By Archibald Ballantyne. Crown 8vo. 8s. 6d.

THE JOCKEY CLUB AND ITS FOUNDERS. By Robert Black, M.A., Author of 'Horse Racing in France,' &c. Crown 8vo. 10s. 6d.

THE LIFE AND LETTERS OF ROBERT BROWNING. By Mrs. Sutherland Orr. With Portrait, and Steel Engraving of Mr. Browning's Study in De Vere Gardens. Second Edition. Crown 8vo. 12s. 6d.

ENGLISH PROSE: its Elements, History and Usage. By John Earle, M.A., Rector of Swanswick, formerly Fellow and Tutor of Oriel College, Professor of Anglo-Saxon in the University of Oxford, Author of 'The Philology of the English Tongue,' &c. 8vo. 16s.

THE HISTORIC NOTE-BOOK; with an Appendix of Battles. By the Rev. E. Cobham Brewer, LL.D., Author of 'The Dictionary of Phrase and Fable,' 'The Reader's Handbook,' &c. Crown 8vo. over 1,000 pp., 7s. 6d.

GEOLOGICAL OBSERVATIONS ON THE VOLCANIC ISLANDS AND PARTS OF SOUTH AMERICA, visited during the Voyage of H.M.S. 'Beagle.' By Charles Darwin, M.A., F.R.S. Third Edition. With Maps and Illustrations. Crown 8vo. 12s. 6d.

THE STRUCTURE AND DISTRIBUTION OF CORAL REEFS. By Charles Darwin, M.A., F.R.S., F.G.S. With an Introduction by Professor T. G. Bonney, D.Sc., F.R.S., F.G.S. Third Edition. Crown 8vo. 8s. 6d.

HAYTI; or, the Black Republic. By Sir Spenser St. John, K.C.M.G., formerly Her Majesty's Minister Resident and Consul-General in Hayti, now Her Majesty's Special Envoy to Mexico. Second Edition, revised. With a Map. Large crown 8vo. 8s. 6d.

THE REIGN OF QUEEN VICTORIA: a Survey of Fifty Years of Progress. Edited by T. Humphry Ward. 2 vols. 8vo. 32s.

A COLLECTION OF LETTERS OF W. M. THACKERAY, 1847-1855. With Portraits and Reproductions of Letters and Drawings. Second Edition. Imperial 8vo. 12s. 6d.

A JOURNAL KEPT BY DICK DOYLE IN THE YEAR 1840. Illustrated by several hundred Sketches by the Author. With an Introduction by J. Hungerford Pollen, and a Portrait. Second Edition. Demy 4to. 21s.

LIFE OF FRANK BUCKLAND. By his Brother-in-Law, George C. Bompas, Editor of 'Notes and Jottings from Animal Life.' With a Portrait. Crown 8vo. 5s.; gilt edges. 6s.

NOTES AND JOTTINGS FROM ANIMAL LIFE. By the late Frank Buckland. With Illustrations. Crown 8vo. 5s.; gilt edges, 6s.

THE INGENIOUS GENTLEMAN, DON QUIXOTE OF LA MANCHA. By Miguel De Cervantes Saavedra. A Translation, with Introduction and Notes, by John Ormsby, Translator of 'The Poem of the Cid.' Complete in 4 vols. 8vo. £2. 10s.

SHAKESPEARE. Certain Selected Plays Abridged for the Use of the Young. By Samuel Brandram, M.A. Oxon. Fourth and Cheaper Edition. Large crown 8vo. 5s.
Titles of the Plays:—The Merchant of Venice—Romeo and Juliet—A Midsummer Night's Dream—Much Ado about Nothing—Twelfth Night—As You Like it—Hamlet—Macbeth—The Tempest.
*** Also the 9 Plays separately, crown 8vo. neatly bound in cloth limp, price 6d. each.

SHAKSPEARE COMMENTARIES. By Dr. G. G. Gervinus, Professor at Heidelberg. Translated, under the Author's superintendence, by F. E. Bunnett. With a Preface by F. J. Furnivall. Fifth Edition. 8vo. 14s.

THE EARLY LIFE OF SAMUEL ROGERS. By P. W. Clayden, Author of 'Rogers and his Contemporaries,' 'Samuel Sharpe, Egyptologist and Translator of the Bible,' &c. Large post 8vo. 12s. 6d.

London: SMITH, ELDER, & CO., 15 Waterloo Place.

AN AGNOSTIC'S APOLOGY; and other Essays. By LESLIE STEPHEN. Large crown 8vo. 10s. 6d.

LIFE OF HENRY FAWCETT. By LESLIE STEPHEN. With 2 Steel Portraits. Fifth Edition. Large crown 8vo. 12s. 6d.

HOURS IN A LIBRARY. By LESLIE STEPHEN. New, Revised, Rearranged, and Cheaper Edition, with additional Chapters. 3 volumes. Crown 8vo. 6s. each.

A HISTORY OF ENGLISH THOUGHT IN THE EIGHTEENTH CENTURY. Second Edition. By LESLIE STEPHEN. 2 vols. demy 8vo. 28s.

THE SCIENCE OF ETHICS: an Essay upon Ethical Theory, as Modified by the Doctrine of Evolution. By LESLIE STEPHEN. Demy 8vo. 16s.

RENAISSANCE IN ITALY. By JOHN ADDINGTON SYMONDS. THE REVIVAL OF LEARNING. Second Edition. Demy 8vo. 16s. THE FINE ARTS. Second Edition. Demy 8vo. 16s. THE CATHOLIC REACTION. 2 vols. demy 8vo. 32s.

SHAKSPERE'S PREDECESSORS IN THE ENGLISH DRAMA. By JOHN ADDINGTON SYMONDS. Demy 8vo. 16s.

LITERATURE AND DOGMA: an Essay towards a better Apprehension of the Bible. By MATTHEW ARNOLD. Popular Edition, with a New Preface. Crown 8vo. 2s. 6d.

GOD AND THE BIBLE: a Sequel to 'Literature and Dogma.' By MATTHEW ARNOLD. Popular Edition, with a new Preface. Crown 8vo. 2s. 6d.

ST. PAUL AND PROTESTANTISM; with other Essays. By MATTHEW ARNOLD. Popular Edition, with a new Preface. Crown 8vo. 2s. 6d.

CULTURE AND ANARCHY: an Essay in Political and Social Criticism. By MATTHEW ARNOLD. Popular Edition. Crown 8vo. 2s. 6d.

IRISH ESSAYS, AND OTHERS. By MATTHEW ARNOLD. Popular Edition. Crown 8vo. 2s. 6d.

ON THE STUDY OF CELTIC LITERATURE. By MATTHEW ARNOLD. Popular Edition. Crown 8vo. 2s. 6d.

THE STORY OF GOETHE'S LIFE. By GEORGE HENRY LEWES. Second Edition. Crown 8vo. 7s. 6d.

THE LIFE OF GOETHE. By GEORGE HENRY LEWES. Fourth Edition, Revised according to the latest Documents, with Portrait. 8vo. 16s.

LIBERTY, EQUALITY, FRATERNITY. By Sir JAMES FITZJAMES STEPHEN, K.C.S.I. Second Edition, with a new Preface. Demy 8vo. 14s.

UNDERGROUND RUSSIA. Revolutionary Profiles and Sketches from Life. By STEPNIAK, formerly Editor of 'Zemlia i Volia' (Land and Liberty). With a Preface by PETER LAVROFF. Translated from the Italian. Third Edition. Crown 8vo. 6s.

THE WESTERN AVERNUS; or, Toil and Travel in Further North America. By MORLEY ROBERTS. Crown 8vo. 7s. 6d.

LIFE AND WRITINGS OF JOSEPH MAZZINI. In 6 vols. Crown 8vo. 4s. 6d. each.

THE SCIENTIFIC SPIRIT OF THE AGE; and other Pleas and Discussions, including an Essay on 'THE EDUCATION OF THE EMOTIONS.' By FRANCES POWER COBBE. Crown 8vo. 6s.

EXTRACTS FROM THE WRITINGS OF W. M. THACKERAY. Chiefly Philosophical and Reflective. Cheap Edition. Fcp. 8vo. 2s. 6d.

LIBERALISM IN RELIGION; and other Sermons. By W. PAGE ROBERTS, M.A., Minister of St. Peter's, Vere Street, London. Second Edition. Crown 8vo. 6s.

By the same Author.

LAW AND GOD. Fifth Edition. Crown 8vo. 5s.

London: SMITH, ELDER, & CO., 15 Waterloo Place.

W. M. THACKERAY'S WORKS.

THE EDITION DE LUXE. Twenty-six Volumes, imperial 8vo. Containing 248 Steel Engravings, 1,620 Wood Engravings, and 88 Coloured Illustrations. The steel and wood engravings are all printed on real China paper. The NUMBER of COPIES PRINTED is LIMITED to ONE THOUSAND, each copy being numbered. The work can only be obtained through booksellers, who will furnish information regarding terms, &c.

THE STANDARD EDITION. Twenty-six Volumes, large 8vo, 10s. 6d. each. This Edition contains some of Mr. Thackeray's writings which had not been previously collected, with many additional Illustrations. It has been printed from new type, on fine paper; and, with the exception of the Édition de Luxe, it is the largest and handsomest edition that has been published.

THE LIBRARY EDITION. Twenty-four Volumes, large crown 8vo. handsomely bound in cloth, price £9; or half-russia, marbled edges, £13. 13s. With Illustrations by the Author, RICHARD DOYLE, and FREDERICK WALKER.

⁎ *The Volumes are sold separately, in cloth, price 7s. 6d. each.*

THE POPULAR EDITION. Thirteen Volumes, crown 8vo. with Frontispiece to each volume, scarlet cloth, gilt top, price £3. 5s.; or half-morocco, gilt, price £5. 10s.

⁎ *The Volumes are sold separately, in green cloth, price 5s. each.*

CHEAPER ILLUSTRATED EDITION. Twenty-six Volumes, crown 8vo. bound in cloth, price £4. 11s.; or handsomely bound in half-morocco, price £8. 8s. Containing nearly all the small Woodcut Illustrations of the former Editions and many new Illustrations by Eminent Artists.

THIS EDITION CONTAINS ALTOGETHER 1,773 ILLUSTRATIONS.

By the AUTHOR; LUKE FILDES, A.R.A.; Lady BUTLER (Miss Elizabeth Thompson); GEORGE DU MAURIER; RICHARD DOYLE; FREDERICK WALKER, A.R.A.; GEORGE CRUIKSHANK; JOHN LEECH; FRANK DICKSEE; LINDLEY SAMBOURNE; F. BARNARD; E. J. WHEELER; F. A. FRASER; CHARLES KEENE; R. B. WALLACE; J. P. ATKINSON; W. J. WEBB; T. R. MACQUOID; M. FITZGERALD; W. RALSTON; JOHN COLLIER; H. FURNISS; G. G. KILBURNE, &c. &c. &c.

⁎ *The Volumes are sold separately, in cloth, price 3s. 6d. each.*

THE POCKET EDITION. Twenty-seven Volumes. Price 1s. 6d. each, in half-cloth, cut or uncut edges; or 1s. in paper cover.

⁎ *The Set of 27 Volumes can be had in a Handsome Ebonised Case, price £2. 12s. 6d. They are also supplied, elegantly bound in cloth, with gilt top, as follows:*

| THE NOVELS. 13 volumes, in gold-lettered cloth case, 21s. | THE MISCELLANIES. 14 volumes, in gold-lettered cloth case, 21s. |

W. M. THACKERAY'S LETTERS.

A COLLECTION OF LETTERS OF W. M. THACKERAY, 1847-1855. With Portraits and Reproductions of Letters and Drawings. Second Edition. Imperial 8vo. 12s. 6d.

BALLADS. By WILLIAM MAKEPEACE THACKERAY. With a Portrait of the Author, and 56 Illustrations by the Author; Lady BUTLER (Miss Elizabeth Thompson); GEORGE DU MAURIER; JOHN COLLIER; H. FURNISS; G. G. KILBURNE; M. FITZGERALD; and J. P. ATKINSON. Printed on toned paper by Clay, Sons, & Taylor; and elegantly bound in cloth, gilt edges, by Burn. Small 4to. 16s.

W. M. THACKERAY'S SKETCHES.

THE ORPHAN OF PIMLICO, and other Sketches, Fragments, and Drawings. By WILLIAM MAKEPEACE THACKERAY. Copied by a process that gives a faithful reproduction of the originals. With a Preface and Editorial Notes by Miss Thackeray. A New Edition, in a new style of binding, bevelled boards, gilt edges, royal 4to. price One Guinea.

London: SMITH, ELDER, & CO., 15 Waterloo Place.

www.ingramcontent.com/pod-product-compliance
Lightning Source LLC
Chambersburg PA
CBHW021919180426
43199CB00032B/1043